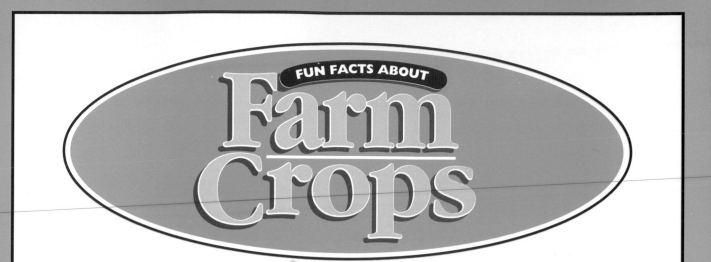

FUN FACTS ABOUT
Farm Crops

Written by
Carol Benanti
& Ray H. Miller

Illustrated by
Andrew Crabtree

The ERTL Company, Inc. would like to thank the following associations, companies, individuals, and universities who helped make Fun Facts About Farm Crops possible:

Corel Corporation; Farm Safety 4 Just Kids; George Horvath of the Florida Department of Citrus; B.W. Hoffmann; Ken Kashian of the Illinois Farm Bureau; Mary Humann of the National Honey Board; Cooperative Extension Service/Michigan State University; and Stan Harrison of the U.S. Department of Agriculture

PHOTO CREDITS

COREL PROFESSIONAL PHOTOGRAPHS

Page 5 photo of tulip field courtesy of Corel Corp.
Page 7 photo of corn field courtesy of Corel Corp.
Page 15 inset photo of potatoes courtesy of Corel Corp.
Page 25 inset photo of carrots courtesy of Corel Corp.
Page 27 photo of lettuce field courtesy of Corel Corp.

FLORIDA DEPARTMENT OF CITRUS

Page 21 photo of orange grove courtesy of FLA. Dept. of Citrus.
Page 21 inset photo of oranges courtesy of FLA. Dept. of Citrus.

B.W. HOFFMANN

Page 9 photo of wheat field courtesy of B.W. Hoffmann.
Page 9 inset photo of wheat shock courtesy of B.W. Hoffmann.
Page 29 inset photo of pumpkin courtesy of B.W. Hoffman.
Page 29 photo of pumpkins courtesy of B.W. Hoffmann.

ILLINOIS FARM BUREAU

Page 7 inset photo of ear of corn courtesy of Illinois Farm Bureau.
Page 19 photo of sunflower field courtesy of Illinois Farm Bureau.
Cover photos of sunflower field courtesy of Illinois Farm Bureau.

NATIONAL HONEY BOARD

Page 17 photo of honey jars courtesy of National Honey Board.
Page 17 photo of honey bee courtesy of National Honey Board.

MICHIGAN STATE UNIVERSITY

Page 11 photo of broccoli field courtesy of Michigan State University/Cooperative Extension Service.

U.S. DEPARTMENT OF AGRICULTURE

Cover (apples) photo courtesy of U.S.D.A.
Page 11 inset photo of broccoli courtesy of U.S.D.A.
Page 13 photo of cotton field courtesy of U.S.D.A.
Page 13 inset photo of cotton plant courtesy of U.S.D.A.
Page 15 photo of potato field courtesy of U.S.D.A.
Page 19 inset photo of sunflower courtesy of U.S.D.A.
Page 23 photo of apple orchard courtesy of U.S.D.A.
Page 23 inset photo of apples courtesy of U.S.D.A.
Page 25 photo of carrot field courtesy of U.S.D.A.
Page 27 photo of lettuce head courtesy of U.S.D.A.

Printed in the U.S.A.
ISBN 1-887327-02-9
10 9 8 7 6 5 4 3 2 1

TABLE OF CONTENTS

DOWN ON THE FARM

Fun Facts About Farm Crops will show you a side of farm crops you've never seen. This book takes a look at some ordinary farm crops with some extraordinary characteristics. Whether it's sunflowers, sugar cane, cotton, or cauliflower, you'll find out that there's more to farm crops than planting seeds and picking fruit.

What vegetable was once worth its weight in gold? Which crop plant is used to make everything from margarine to make-up, fabric to fertilizer? What do oranges have to do with the "Fountain of Youth?" Keep turning the pages of *Fun Facts About Farm Crops* to find out the answers to these questions, and much, much more.

CORN

Many people don't realize that when they are eating corn, they are really eating the seed of the corn plant. Peas, kidney beans, and lima beans are also considered *seed* vegetables. Corn seeds are now being used in ways you could never imagine. Many industries use corn in a variety of products. It is used in vitamins, fuel, and in the production of plastics. With over 3,500 different uses, corn is a very valuable crop. Let's see just how valuable corn is.

SPACE-AGE CORN

The United States produces more corn to feed animals than any other grain. In 1993 and 1994, corn production reached new heights, with over 10 billion bushels harvested. If every ear of that corn could be stacked end to end, it would be long enough to reach from Earth to Mars.

PICTURE-PERFECT CORN

The next time you run out of film for your camera, consider heading to the nearest cornfield. That's not as crazy as it sounds. One of the many ways to use corn is in the manufacturing of photographic film. Smile at the camera and say "Corn!"

CORNY GOLF TEES

Golf courses often become littered with broken wooden golf tees. Greenskeepers have to pick these up by hand. This practice may soon change. Golf tees are now being made from a plastic whose main ingredient is cornstarch. Greenskeepers won't have to worry about these tees – they're biodegradable.

This means that they are able to break down into tiny bits by natural process.

BUTTER OR PLAIN?

For years corn has played a major role in the movie industry. Not as a leading actor, but as popcorn. Popcorn made at home or at movie theaters is made from a variety of corn called popcorn. A bushel contains about 72,800 kernels of corn. If the kernels in just one bushel of corn were popped into popcorn, it would easily overflow two bathtubs. Think about all the movies you could watch from your bathtub with that much popcorn!

WHEAT

Wheat, a simple grass, is used to feed millions of people around the world. There are many classes of wheat, but the four that we use most are *hard red winter wheat*, which provides us with three-quarters of all our breads; *soft red winter wheat*, which is used to make cookies and cakes; *durum wheat*, which is used to make pasta; and *hard red spring wheat*, which is used to make Italian and French breads. Here are some other things about wheat that will surprise you.

LAND OF THE LOAVES

In 1993, wheat farmers harvested over 2 billion bushels of wheat, which was enough to bake over 169 billion loaves of bread. That would be enough loaves to fill more than all the land in the state of Delaware with loaves of bread.

FAST FOOD

If you were working in a bakery, and someone called to say they were picking up 13 loaves of bread, or a "baker's dozen," in less than a half hour, would you tell them there's not enough time? Not if you worked for a company called Wheat Montana in Three Forks, Montana. On August 29, 1991, they produced 13 loaves of bread from raw wheat in a little over 21 minutes.

HARVEST KING

A combine can harvest about 45 bushels of wheat in one hour. That would sound like a lot of wheat to almost anyone except Max Louder. On July 29, 1990, Max broke a world record for the most wheat harvested in one hour. Using a Case International combine, Max raced through almost 13 acres in less than one hour. The total wheat harvested was almost 2,000 bushels, or 54 tons.

WHEAT MECHANICS

For thousands of years, farmers harvested wheat by hand, and tied it into bundles to be *threshed*. Threshing removes the kernel, or grain, of wheat from the stalk. Threshing used to be done by letting cattle trample over the stalks. The wheat *chaff* would then blow away, leaving only the grain. In the late 1820's, it would take a farmer over 60 hours to plow the soil, plant the seed, and cut and thresh one acre of wheat. Machines were eventually built to harvest and thresh the wheat. Today the same amount of work can be done in less than three hours.

BROCCOLI & CAULIFLOWER

Have you ever eaten a "flower bud" vegetable? Broccoli is a flower bud vegetable and so is its cousin, cauliflower. Mark Twain, a famous American writer, called cauliflower "the cabbage with a college education." Do you suppose it's because cauliflower has the same vitamins as cabbage, but more of each? Or is it because it has such a "brainy" look? Cauliflower was once grown only in home gardens. Now it's grown in large fields. Let's see how "smart" these cousins really are.

BEDS OF BROCCOLI

If production is any sign, it seems people are enjoying broccoli these days.

The United States produced over 1 billion pounds of broccoli in 1993. Transporting that much broccoli would be quite a job. If everyone living in the city of Minneapolis, Minnesota, owned a pickup truck, and they filled the bed of every truck with broccoli, they could get the job done.

CAULIFLOWER CRUNCH?

Even though cauliflower may not survive a frost as well as broccoli, it doesn't seem to grow very well in hot weather either.

Despite how finicky cauliflower is to grow, the United States still produced over 665 million pounds of it in 1993. That's enough cauliflower for everybody in the U.S. to eat almost 3 pounds.

HEADS UP!

An average head of broccoli is 6 to 7 inches wide. If all the heads of broccoli harvested in the United States in 1993 were laid side to side in a straight line starting at the South Pole heading north, that line of broccoli would circle Earth almost five times.

EDIBLE FLOWERS

Did you ever think you would eat a bowl of flower buds? That's what you're eating when you have broccoli and cauliflower for dinner. These vegetables have heads that are really clusters of flower buds. Both are loaded with vitamins and minerals that help make your bones strong, plus they may help fight cold symptoms when you are feeling "under the weather." The next time you want to bring flowers to someone you like, and you want to make them feel healthier, you could bring them broccoli or cauliflower!

COTTON

Of all the plants that we use for fiber, cotton provides us with the most products, including bookbinding, typewriter ribbons, and furniture fabric. When cotton is treated with chemicals, it is used to make products like paper, plastics, and even the vinyl records that play on a record player. *Jute*, another type of fibrous plant, is used to make rope and carpeting, as well as burlap to cover the cotton. Keep reading and find out more fun facts about cotton.

THE STATE OF COTTON

The United States produced nearly 4 million tons of cotton in 1992. Just over 11 million acres of land were used to grow that cotton. That would be like planting cotton fields over Vermont and Massachusetts.

BUNDLE UP!

People in the United States use about 3.5 billion pounds of cotton every year. How would you like to wear 14 pounds of 100% cotton shirts all at once? That's the average of how much cotton each person in the U.S. uses in one year.

BIG-TIME BALES

When cotton is harvested, it is packed in square or round bundles called bales. Farmers in the U.S. produce about 15 million bales of cotton every year and each one weighs roughly 480 pounds. It takes about 6 yards of jute to cover each giant bale, and 6 steel ties to hold the bale together.

You can get an idea of how big these bales are the next time you're hungry – one cotton bale is about as big as your refrigerator!

COTTON CLEANER

In 1793 Eli Whitney invented the cotton gin, which cleaned cotton by removing the seeds from the fiber. Whitney's invention made it possible for one person to clean as much cotton as 50 people could by hand. The cotton gin not only cleaned cotton, but it also provided an easy way to gather the seeds. Cottonseed is crushed to make oil. That oil is used to make many things, including margarine, salad oil, cosmetics, and cattle feed. Today, cotton is a major industry, and we owe it all to Eli Whitney and his cotton gin.

POTATOES

Potatoes are from a unique group of vegetables called *tubers*. Tubers are actually the specialized underground stems of certain plants. Yams are also tubers. In 1992, the U.S. harvested over 20 million tons of potatoes, which could make 800 billion french fries. The amount of ketchup needed to put on that gigantic order of fries would fill over 6,000 average-sized swimming pools! Here are some more amazing facts about potatoes.

SUPER-DUPER SWEET POTATO

Think you could feed all of your friends with one potato? In 1982 O. Harrison of Kite, Georgia, could have. Harrison grew a giant sweet potato that weighed over 40 pounds. This super-duper sweet potato would have been more than enough for 80 people to share.

PEELING OUT

Would you believe a potato could be peeled in 1½ seconds? You would if you were a resident of Shelley, Idaho, on September 19, 1992.

Potato skins were flying at the 64th Annual Idaho Spud Day celebration when five people peeled over 1,000 pounds of potatoes in 45 minutes. All those potatoes could have made mashed potatoes for 2,000 people.

SOME CHIP WITH YOUR DIP?

It's fun to reach into a bag of chips and pull out the biggest chip you can find. On April 19, 1990, the

Pringles plant in Jackson, Tennessee, gave new meaning to the word "big" when they produced a chip that measured almost 24 inches x 14 inches. This giant chip was made from potato flour. If you wanted to spread dip on that chip, you'd need a container of dip the size of a half-gallon carton of ice cream!

14K GOLD POTATOES

Potatoes were once worth their weight in gold – literally. People from all over the world came to California to pan for gold during the famous gold rush of 1849. According to a potato expert at the Potato Expo in Blackfoot, Idaho, many of these people became sick along the way and needed vitamin C to help make them feel better. Because potatoes are so high in vitamin C, the gold-rushers would actually trade gold, ounce per ounce, for potatoes. Now those were some expensive spuds!

SUGAR

Sugar helps make our lives sweeter. It is one of the main ingredients in candy, jelly, soda, ice cream, and chocolate. Because we're a nation that loves its sweets, farmers in the U.S. produce about 6.5 million tons of sugar every year. Most of this sugar comes from sugar cane or sugar beets. Other sweeteners produced in the U.S. include honey, maple syrup and molasses. If you love sweets, then these next few facts are for you.

PILES OF PANCAKES

Most of the maple syrup in the U.S. comes from Vermont and New York. New York alone produces an average of 315,000 gallons each year. That's enough syrup for everyone in the states of Arkansas, Louisiana, Mississippi, Alabama, and Georgia to enjoy syrup on their pancakes one morning.

HOME SWEET HOME

The most sugar beets ever grown on one acre of land was 62.4 tons. This sweet crop was grown

by Andy Christenson and Jon Giannini in Salinas Valley, California. Their one acre of sugar beets could have produced 31,200 pounds of *sucrose*, or table sugar. That's enough sugar to sweeten a glass of iced tea for everyone living in the state of Utah.

A CHERRY ON TOP?

The people at Palm Dairies Ltd., in Alberta, Canada, must have had a sweet tooth on July 24, 1988. They made a sundae that weighed almost 55,000 pounds. It was made with over 44,689 pounds of ice cream, 9,688 pounds of syrup, and 537 pounds of toppings. That sundae was as heavy as 20 hippopotamuses. It doesn't get much sweeter than that.

BUSLOADS OF HONEY

Flowers are a sweet gift to give someone, but did you know that they actually help make honey? Honey is the end result of honey bees "sipping" nectar from the flower and carrying it back to the bee hive. Each honey bee carries the nectar in their tiny *honey stomach*. It's hard work, but it pays off. About 200 million pounds of honey are produced in the U.S. every year, with most of it coming from Florida, California, and South Dakota. All that honey equals the weight of about 10,000 school buses full of elementary students.

SUNFLOWERS
AND OTHER TYPES OF NUTS

Giant sunflowers turn to face the sun during the day, and add bright orange and yellow bursts of color to any farm. Sunflowers, and many other kinds of nuts, are valued for their dry, delicious seeds. The United States is one of the leading producers of nuts, and peanuts is the number one nut crop. The biggest sunflower crops in the U.S. are in Minnesota, North Dakota, South Dakota, and Kansas. Get ready for some more nutty facts.

PEANUT BUTTER PARTY
The United States produced over 3 billion pounds of peanuts in 1993. About half of those peanuts were used to make peanut butter, which would be enough to make almost 23 billion peanut butter and jelly sandwiches. That's about 89 sandwiches for every person in the U.S.

HEAVY-DUTY SUNFLOWER SEEDS
One sunflower can grow to be a foot wide and have as many as 1,000 tiny seeds. The U.S. produced nearly 2.6 billion pounds

of sunflower seeds in 1993 alone. All of those tiny sunflower seeds together would weigh as much as over 43,000 giant four-wheel drive tractors.

PIE PATROL
An average pecan tree can produce up to 500 pounds of pecans every year, and all of the pecan trees in the United States pro-duced 365 million pounds of pecans in 1993. Most of

them were grown in Georgia, Texas, Louisiana, and New Mexico. Those pecans could have made 730 million pecan pies. That would be enough to deliver three to almost every person living in the United States.

SUPER SEEDS

If you were stranded on an island and the only plants growing there were sunflowers, you probably wouldn't have to worry about food. Medical experts claim that sunflower seeds are so full of vitamins, a person could almost survive from eating just them and nothing else. Sunflower seeds help strengthen poor eyesight and help make fingernails grow stronger. Besides being good for us, sunflower oil is sometimes even used as a replacement for diesel fuel in cars and trucks. If only sunflowers could be made into a boat to get off that island!

ORANGES & OTHER CITRUS

Oranges are the leading citrus fruit grown today, but grapefruit, tangerines, tangelos, lemons, and limes are popular too. Together they contribute 2 billion dollars to California's economy each year. Why is this group of fruit so popular? Besides being packed with vitamins B and C, maybe the biggest reason why citrus is a top crop is because it's so delicious. Let's look at some more juicy facts about oranges and the rest of the citrus family.

WHOLE LOTTA LEMON

Talk about tart. The largest lemon ever grown was by C. and D. Knutzen of Whittier, California, in 1993. Their lemon weighed 8 pounds 8 ounces. That large lemon could have made 32 glasses of lemonade – enough for each student in an average elementary school classroom!

OODLES OF ORANGES

All the oranges harvested in the United States in one year could produce 275 million gallons of orange juice. If all

that juice was poured into 8-ounce glasses and stacked on top of the other, they would reach from the ground floor to the top of the 110-story Sears Tower, the world's tallest building, almost 6,000 times.

BOWLING BALL BREAKFAST

What would you do if 10 people dropped by unexpectedly for breakfast and all you had was one grapefruit? J. and A. Sosnow of Tucson, Arizona, would

simply cut their grapefruit into ten pieces and serve it up. The Sosnow's grew a grapefruit that weighed 6 pounds 8 ounces – the weight of a lightweight bowling ball.

ORANGE YOU GLAD?

In 1513, Spanish explorer, Ponce de Leon came to America looking for the "Fountain of Youth." He and his fellow explorers brought the first citrus plants to this country. Florida's weather was the perfect climate for citrus, and by 1579, the first oranges were harvested near St. Augustine on Florida's east coast. By 1800, the St. Johns River was lined with orange groves. Thanks to Ponce de Leon's search for eternal youth, there are 80 million citrus trees growing on over 700,000 acres in the state of Florida today.

APPLES
& OTHER FRUIT

Each year, the U.S. produces over 190 million bushels of apples, which are worth about 1 billion dollars. Half are eaten fresh off the tree, the rest go into apple sauce, pies, and other fruit dishes. Americans also go bananas over other fruits. Each year they eat 11 billion bananas. Over 5 million tons of grapes are produced in California yearly. It's quite obvious fruit is popular in America. What do you think of these fruity facts?

NOW THAT'S A-PEELING!
An apple peel that is stretched across the length of two basketball courts must come from a huge apple, right? Actually, no. One apple that was skillfully peeled in 1976 by Kathy Wafler weighed only 20 ounces. She peeled her apple for 11 hours and 30 minutes in Rochester, New York. Her unbroken apple peel was over 172 feet long from end to end.

GOING BANANAS
A group of people in Selinsgrove, Pennsylvania, must have had a *big* craving for dessert on April 30, 1988. They made a banana

split that was over 4½ miles long – the longest banana split on record. This tremendous dessert would have reached halfway up the coast of Miami Beach.

NICE CATCH!
It seemed like a simple game of catch between James Deady and Paul Tavilla in Boston, Massachusetts, on May 27, 1992. But James didn't throw a ball, he threw a grape. And Paul didn't catch the grape in his hands, he caught it in his mouth. A more amazing thing is that the high-flying grape was thrown a distance of over 327 feet. That's longer than the length of a professional football field!

AN APPLE A DAY...

"An apple a day keeps the doctor away." No one knows who made this famous quote, but many people agree with it. Apples are high in vitamins which improve vision and help keep your skin healthy. If you took the doctor's advice and ate one apple a day for a year, that would be enough apples to fill more than two bushels. Apples have also played a part in American history. In the early 1800's, a pioneer apple planter named John Chapman planted apple trees throughout Ohio and Indiana. You may know him as "Johnny Appleseed."

CARROTS & OTHER ROOTS

Carrots are one of the most popular vegetables in the world. These crisp, sweet vegetables are really the *roots* of the carrot plants. Carrots are farmed from seeds that are planted in rows of raised beds. These beds provide deep, loose soil that help the carrot roots grow long and straight. Carrots are harvested by machines that lift them out of the ground and pull the tops off. Here's a few things you probably don't know about carrots and other root vegetables.

CAPTIVATING CARROTS

There were over 3 billion pounds of carrots grown in the United States in 1993. The average carrot measures between 6 and 9 inches long. If all those carrots harvested in 1993 were laid end to end, they would circle Earth over 114 times.

RIP ROARIN' RADISH

Florida, California, and Ohio produce the most radishes in the United States. These small red root vegetables normally weigh from under 1 ounce to over 2 pounds. That wasn't the case with the

Litterini family of South Australia. In 1992, they grew a radish that weighed 37 pounds 15 ounces.

That's almost 1,000 times as big as a regular radish. A radish that large could be sliced for 4,000 salads!

BODACIOUS BEET

In the United States, the leading producers of beets are New York and Wisconsin. However, the biggest beet ever was grown in California in 1984, by

R. Meyer. This bodacious beet weighed over 45 pounds, which is as much as an average five-year-old child.

CARROT COUSINS

You'd be amazed to know how many different relatives the carrot has. The herb *anise* is a member of the carrot family and is used to flavor licorice and cough drops. Celery is also a member of the carrot family, along with *caraway*. Caraway produces tiny seeds that are used in rye bread. Another herb called *Queen Anne's Lace* is also a member of the carrot family. This herb is grown in Europe and Asia and is called "wild carrot." Queen Anne's Lace grows 3 feet tall and has stems with clusters of white or pink flowers.

LETTUCE
& LEAFY VEGETABLES

The Greeks and Romans enjoyed lettuce in their salads back in 700 B.C., and fresh lettuce is still the main ingredient in most salads today. Besides being crisp and refreshing, leafy vegetables such as lettuce, brussels sprouts, cabbage, and spinach are very healthy foods. And while it won't replace the toothbrush, chewing lettuce leaves can help to clean your teeth and gums. "Lettuce" tell you more about leafy vegetables.

CRAZY FOR KRAUT
The United States produced over 2 billion pounds of cabbage in 1993, and about 54 million pounds of it was used to make sauer-

kraut. That would be enough sauerkraut to put on 12 hot dogs for each person living in the state of Texas.

SPIRALING SPINACH

Spinach has the most protein of all the leafy vegetables, so it's not surprising why a famous cartoon sailor gained superhuman strength from eating just one can of spinach.

It also may be part of why it is so popular. The United States produced over 500 million pounds of spinach in 1993. That's enough to fill about 264 million cans.

If all those cans of spinach were laid end to end, they would almost reach around Earth.

HOLD THE LETTUCE?

There were over 6.5 billion pounds of lettuce produced in the United States in 1993. If all the people in the U.S. were to split up that much lettuce evenly, each person would have a giant salad weighing over 26 pounds.

LETTUCE TALK

If you order a salad these days, it doesn't necessarily mean that you're getting a salad with garden lettuce. The most popular is *iceberg lettuce*. Its leaves curl tightly around the middle to form a round head. There is *leaf lettuce*, which is a thick bunch of leaves. There is also *romaine lettuce*, which is tall and slim. One of the strangest types of lettuce is *celtuce*. This lettuce looks and tastes like a combination of celery and lettuce. The next time someone asks you what kind of salad you want, tell them it's a "toss-up" between iceberg, leaf, and romaine lettuce.

PUMPKINS
& OTHER GOURDS

What do you think of when you see a pumpkin? A Jack-O-Lantern on Halloween? A pumpkin pie on Thanksgiving? You probably don't think of squash or watermelons, but they all belong to the same family, called *gourds*. Gourds grow on bushes or ground vines. Many other important farm crops, such as cucumbers and melons, are also members of the gourd family. Let's look at some gourds that are outstanding in their fields.

PLENTY OF PUMPKIN

Average pumpkins weighing between 15 and 30 pounds obviously weren't big enough for a farmer named Joel Holland. In 1992, Joel grew a 827-pound pumpkin. That giant pumpkin could have filled over 400 pumpkin pies.

HEAVYWEIGHT MELON

Watermelons are grown mainly in Florida, Texas, and Georgia, but a giant watermelon was grown in Arrington, Tennessee. Most watermelons weigh between 5 and 40 pounds, but not

B. Carson's watermelon. It grew to be 262 pounds. That mega-melon was heavier than an average heavyweight boxer.

SCALE SQUASHER

Squash was in America long before the European settlers arrived. The Native Americans called this crop "askutasquash," which means "eaten raw." Today over 40 kinds of squash are grown in the United States. It would be hard to find a squash to compare to the one L. Stellpflug found growing in his Rush, New York, garden in 1990. This gigantic gourd weighed 821 pounds, which is more than the weight of three baby elephants!

PERFECT PATCHMATES

Early European settlers wondered why Native Americans planted pumpkins next to corn. They found that pumpkins and corn grew well in similar conditions. Because pumpkins grow on the ground and corn grows high up on stalks, these two crops were perfect for each other. There's another reason pumpkins are planted next to corn. Raccoons love to eat corn, but when they eat, they like to stand up and keep an eye out for intruders. They'll stay away from the corn because pumpkin leaves block the raccoon's view while they're eating.

HARVEST TIME

Now you have seen how farm crops play a very important role in our lives. In the United States, farm crops are planted on about 465 million acres of land – that's the same amount of land as in Texas, New Mexico, Arizona, and Utah combined. From carrots to cotton, these crops provide us with almost all of our food and much of our clothing. It's no surprise that farm crops are part of one of the most important industries in the world.

We hope that *Fun Facts About Farm Crops* has shown you how fascinating farm crops can be. You'll never look at crops the same way again!

SAFETY TIPS

A farm is a wonderful place to live and visit, but it can be very dangerous. Here are some smart safety tips to keep in mind while on the farm:

1. Never play in crop fields, especially during harvest time. Operators of large machines and equipment may not be able to see or hear you.

2. Tractors are not toys. They have an important job to do. Though it may look like fun, don't ever ride on tractors. There have been many incidents where extra riders have been hurt or even killed after falling off a tractor, even a tractor with a cab.

3. Don't ever play with chemicals. Stay away from containers marked poison with the skull and crossbones. Chemicals should be stored in a locked facility.

Sometimes a farm can seem like a huge playground. But living and working on a farm has many hazards. Farm Safety 4 Just Kids works to prevent farm-related childhood injuries, health risks and fatalities. Contact the organization at 1-800-423-KIDS to learn more about staying safe on the farm. A healthy and safe farm is a happy farm, so always stay alert.

Order The Replica

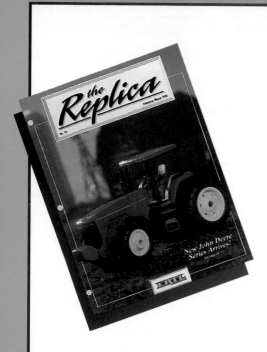

Whether you are a serious collector or just a big fan of farm toys, you should consider a subscription to <u>The Replica</u>. This 4-color, bi-monthly magazine comes to you direct from The Ertl Company. It's full of the latest news about upcoming product releases in die cast farm toys, farm playsets, banks and other Ertl collectibles. And, from time to time, special subscriber-only, exclusive products are offered.

To receive your subscription of <u>The Replica</u>, write to:

The Ertl Company Replica Offer
Dept. 776A Highways 136 & 20
P.O. Box 500, Dyersville, IA 52040-0500

Inside the U.S.A. $10.00 for 1 year and $18.00 for 2 years
Outside the U.S.A. $14.00 for 1 year and $22.00 for 2 years

Farm Safety ❤ Just Kids

For more information on how to stay safe on the farm, call or write:

Farm Safety 4 Just Kids
110 South Chestnut Avenue
P.O. Box 458
Earlham, IA 50072

1-800-423-KIDS or 1-515-758-2827

Fun Facts About Farm Crops was created in cooperation with Farm Safety 4 Just Kids.